MW01194447

Mare Liberum

By Hugo Grotius

Cover Design by Alex Struik

Contents

The Freedom of the Seas, or the Right Which Belongs to the Dutch to take part in the East Indian Trade

TO THE RULERS AND TO THE FREE AND INDEPENDENT NATIONS OF CHRISTENDOM

1608

The delusion is as old as it is detestable with which many men, especially those who by their wealth and power exercise the greatest influence, persuade themselves, or as I rather believe, try to persuade themselves, that justice and injustice are distinguished the one from the other not by their own nature, but in some fashion merely by the opinion and the custom of mankind. Those men therefore think that both the laws and the semblance of equity were devised for the sole purpose of repressing the dissensions and rebellions of those persons born in a subordinate position, affirming meanwhile that they themselves, being placed in a high position, ought to dispense all justice in accordance with their own good pleasure, and that their pleasure ought to be bounded only by their own view of what is expedient. This opinion, absurd and unnatural as it clearly is, has gained considerable currency; but this should by no means occasion surprise, inasmuch as there has to be taken into consideration not only the common fraily of the human race by which we pursue not only vices and their purveyors, but also the arts of flatterers, to whom power is always exposed.

But, on the other hand, there have stood forth in every age independent and wise and devout men able to root out this false doctrine from the minds of the simple, and to convict its advocates of shamelessness. For they showed that God was the founder and ruler of the universe, and especially that being the Father of all mankind, He had not separated human beings, as He had the rest of living things, into different species and various divisions, but had willed them to be of one race and to be known by one name; that furthermore He had given them the same origin, the same structural organism, the ability to look each other in the face, language too, and other means of communication, in order that they all might recognize their natural social bond and kinship. They showed too that He is the supreme Lord and Father of this family; and that for the household or the state which He had thus founded, He had drawn up certain laws not graven on tablets of bronze or stone but written in the minds and on the hearts of every individual, where even the unwilling and the refractory must read them. That these laws were binding on great and small alike; that kings have no more power against them than have the common people against the decrees of the magistrates, than have the magistrates against the edicts of the governors, than have the governors against the ordinances of the kings themselves; nay more, that those very laws themselves of each and every nation and city flow from that Divine source, and from that source receive their sanctity and their majesty.

Now, as there are some things which every man enjoys in common with all other men, and as there are other things which are distinctly his and belong to no one else, just so has nature willed that some of the things which she has created for the use of mankind remain common to all, and that others through the industry and labor of each man become his own. Laws moreover were given to cover both cases so that all men might use common property without prejudice to any one else, and in respect to other things so that each man being content with what he himself owns might refrain from laying his hands on the property of others.

Now since no man can be ignorant of these facts unless he ceases to be a man, and since races blind to all truth except what they receive from the light of nature, have recognized their force, what, O Christian Kings and Nations, ought you to think, and what ought you to do?

If any one thinks it hard that those things are demanded of him which the profession of a religion so sacred requires, the very least obligation of which is to refrain from injustice, certainly every one can know what his own duty is from the very demands he makes of others. There is not one of you who does not openly proclaim that every man is entitled to manage and dispose of his own property; there is not one of you who does not insist that all citizens have equal and indiscriminate right to use rivers and public places; not one of you who does not defend with all his might the freedom of travel and of trade.

If it be thought that the small society which we call a state cannot exist without the application of these principles (and certainly it cannot), why will not those same principles be necessary to uphold the social structure of the whole human race and to maintain the harmony thereof? If any one rebels against these principles of law and order you are justly indignant, and you even decree punishments in proportion to the magnitude of the offense, for no other reason than that a government cannot be tranquil where trespasses of that sort are allowed. If king act unjustly and violently against king, and nation against nation, such action involves a disturbance of the peace of that universal state, and constitutes a trespass against the supreme Ruler, does it not? There is however this difference: just as the lesser magistrates judge the common people, and as you judge the magistrates, so the King of the universe has laid upon you the command to take cognizance of the trespasses of all other men, and to punish them; but He has reserved for

Himself the punishment of your own trespasses. But although He reserves to himself the final punishment, slow and unseen but none the less inevitable, yet He appoints to intervene in human affairs two judges whom the luckiest of sinners does not escape, namely, Conscience, or the innate estimation of oneself, and Public Opinion, or the estimation of others. These two tribunals are open to those who are debarred from all others; to these the powerless appeal; in them are defeated those who are wont to win by might, those who put no bounds to their presumption, those who consider cheap anything bought at the price of human blood, those who defend injustice by injustice, men whose wickedness is so manifest that they must needs be condemned by the unanimous judgment of the good, and cannot be cleared before the bar of their own souls.

To this double tribunal we bring a new case. It is in very truth no petty case such as private citizens are wont to bring against their neighbors about dripping eaves or party walls; nor is it a case such as nations frequently bring against one another about boundary lines or the possession of a river or an island. No! It is a case which concerns practically the entire expanse of the high seas, the right of navigation, the freedom of trade!! Between us and the Spaniards the following points are in dispute: Can the vast, the boundless sea be the appanage of one kingdom alone, and it not the greatest? Can any one nation have the right to prevent other nations which so desire, from selling to one another, from bartering with one another, actually from communicating with one another? Can any nation give away what it never owned, or discover what already belonged to some one else? Does a manifest injustice of long standing create a specific right?

In this controversy we appeal to those jurists among the Spanish themselves who are especially skilled both in divine and human law; we actually invoke the very laws of Spain itself. If that is of no avail, and those whom reason clearly convicts of wrong are induced by greed to maintain that stand, we invoke your majesty, ye Princes, your good faith, ye Peoples, whoever and wherever ye may be.

It is not an involved, it is not an intricate question that I am raising. It is not a question of ambiguous points of theology which seem to be wrapped in the deepest obscurity, which have been debated already so long and with such heat, that wise men are almost convinced that truth is never so rarely found as when assent thereto is forced. It is not a question of the status of our government and of independence not won by arms but restored. On this point those can reach a right decision who have an accurate knowledge of the ancestral laws and hereditary customs of the people of the Netherlands, and who have recognized that their state is not a kingdom illegally founded but is a government based upon law. In this matter, however, just judges no longer compelled to subordinate their convictions have been persuaded; the public authority of many nations has entirely satisfied those who were seeking a precedent; and the admissions of our adversaries have left even the foolish and malevolent no room for doubt.

But what I here submit has nothing in common with these matters. It calls for no troublesome investigation. It does not depend upon an interpretation of Holy Writ in which many people find many things they cannot understand, nor upon the decrees of any one nation of which the rest of the world very properly knows nothing.

The law by which our case must be decided is not difficult to find, seeing that it is the same among all nations; and it is easy to understand, seeing that it is innate in every individual and implanted in his mind. Moreover the law to which we appeal is one such as no king ought to deny to his subjects, and one no Christian ought to refuse to a non-Christian. For it is a law derived from nature, the common mother of us all, whose bounty falls on all, and whose sway extends over those who rule nations, and which is held most sacred by those who are most scrupulously just.

Take cognizance of this cause, ye Princes, take cognizance of it, ye Nations! If we are making an unjust demand, you know what your authority and the authority of those of you who are our nearer neighbors has always been so far as we are concerned. Caution us, we will obey. Verily, if we have done any wrong in this our cause, we will not deprecate your wrath, nor even the hatred of the human race. But if we are right, we leave to your sense of righteousness and of fairness what you ought to think about this matter and what course of action you ought to pursue.

If today the custom held of considering that everything pertaining to mankind pertained also to one's self, we should surely live in a much more peaceable world. For the presumptuousness of many would abate, and those who now neglect justice on the pretext of expediency would unlearn the lesson of injustice at their own expense.

We have felt that perhaps we were not entertaining a foolish hope for our cause. At all events we are confident that you will all recognize after duly weighing the facts in the case that the delays to peace can no more be laid to our charge than can the causes of war; and as hitherto you have been indulgent, even favorably disposed to us, we feel sure that you will not only remain in this mind, but be even more friendly to us in the future. Nothing more to be desired than this can come to men who think that the first condition of happiness is good deeds; the second, good repute.

CHAPTER I

By the Law of Nations navigation is free to all persons whatsoever

My intention is to demonstrate briefly and clearly that the Dutch—that is to say, the subjects of the United Netherlands—have the right to sail to the East Indies, as they are now doing, and to engage in trade with the people there. I shall base my argument on the following most specific and unimpeachable axiom of the Law of Nations, called a primary rule or first principle, the spirit of which is self-evident and immutable, to wit: Every nation is free to travel to every other nation, and to trade with it.

God Himself says this speaking through the voice of nature; and inasmuch as it is not His will to have Nature supply every place with all the necessaries of life, He ordains that some nations excel in one art and others in another. Why is this His will, except it be that He wished human friendships to be engendered by mutual needs and resources, lest individuals deeming themselves entirely sufficient unto themselves should for that very reason be rendered unsociable? So by the decree of divine justice it was brought about that one people should supply the needs of another, in order, as Pliny the Roman writer says, that in this way, whatever has been produced anywhere should seem to have been destined for all. Vergil also sings in this wise:

· "Not every plant on every soil will grow," and in another place: "Let others better mould the running mass Of metals," etc.

Those therefore who deny this law, destroy this most praiseworthy bond of human fellowship, remove the opportunities for doing mutual service, in a word do violence to Nature herself. For do not the ocean, navigable in every direction with which God has encompassed all the earth, and the regular and the occasional winds which blow now from one quarter and now from another, offer sufficient proof that Nature has given to all peoples a right of access to all other peoples? Seneca thinks this is Nature's greatest service, that by the wind she united the widely scattered peoples, and yet did so distribute all her products over the earth that commercial intercourse was a necessity to mankind. Therefore this right belongs equally to all nations. Indeed the most famous jurists extend its application so far as to deny that any state or any ruler can debar foreigners from having access to their subjects and trading with them. Hence is derived that law of hospitality which is of the highest sanctity; hence the complaint of the poet Vergil:

· "What men, what monsters, what inhuman race,
· What laws, what barbarous customs of the place,
· Shut up a desert shore to drowning men,
· And drive us to the cruel seas again."

And:

· "To beg what you without your want may spare—
· The common water, and the common air."

We know that certain wars have arisen over this very matter; such for example as the war of the Megarians against the Athenians, and that of the Bolognese against the Venetians. Again, Victoria holds that the Spaniards could have shown just reasons for making war upon the Aztecs and the Indians in America, more plausible reasons certainly than were alleged, if they really were prevented from traveling or sojourning among those peoples, and were denied the right to share in those things which by the Law of Nations or by Custom are common to all, and finally if they were debarred from trade.

We read of a similar case in the history of Moses, which we find mentioned also in the writings of Augustine, where the Israelites justly smote with the edge of the sword the Amorites because they had denied the Israelites an innocent passage through their territory, a right which according to the Law of Human Society ought in all justice to have been allowed. In defense of this principle Hercules attacked the king of Orchomenus in Boeotia; and the Greeks under their leader Agamemnon waged war against the king of Mysia on the ground that, as Baldus has said, high roads were free by nature. Again, as we read in Tacitus, the Germans accused the Romans of 'preventing all intercourse between them and of closing up to them the rivers and roads, and almost the very air of heaven'. When in days gone by the Christians made crusades against the Saracens, no other pretext was so welcome or so plausible as that they were denied by the infidels free access to the Holy Land.

It follows therefore that the Portuguese, even if they had been sovereigns in those parts to which the Dutch make voyages, would nevertheless be doing them an injury if they should forbid them access to those places and from trading there.

Is it not then an incalculably greater injury for nations which desire reciprocal commercial relations to be debarred therefrom by the acts of those who are sovereigns neither of the nations interested, nor of the element over which their connecting high road runs? Is not that the very cause which for the most part prompts us to execrate robbers and pirates, namely, that they beset and infest our trade routes?

CHAPTER II

The Portuguese have no right by title of discovery to sovereignty over the East Indies to which the Dutch make voyages

The Portuguese are not sovereigns of those parts of the East Indies to which the Dutch sail, that is to say, Java, Ceylon, and many of the Moluccas. This I prove by the incontrovertible argument that no one is sovereign of a thing which he himself has never possessed, and which no one else has ever held in his name. These islands of which we speak, now have and always have had their own kings, their own government, their own laws, and their own legal systems. The inhabitants allow the Portuguese to trade with them, just as they allow other nations the same privilege. Therefore, inasmuch as the Portuguese pay tolls, and obtain leave to trade from the rulers there, they thereby give sufficient proof that they do not go there as sovereigns but as foreigners. Indeed they only reside there on suffrance. And although the title to sovereignty is not sufficient, inasmuch as possession is a prerequisite—for having a thing is quite different from having the right to acquire it—nevertheless I affirm that in those places the Portuguese have no title at all to sovereignty which is not denied them by the opinion of learned men, even of the Spaniards.

First of all, if they say that those lands have come under their jurisdiction as the reward of discovery, THEY LIE, both in law and in fact. For to discover a thing is not only to seize it with the eyes but to take real possession thereof, as Gordian points out in one of his letters. For that reason the Grammarians give the same signification to the expressions 'to find' or 'to discover' and 'to take possession of' or 'to occupy'; and all the Latin with which I am acquainted tells us that the opposite of 'to find' is 'to lose'. However, natural reason itself, the precise words of the law, and the interpretation of the more learned men all show clearly that the act of discovery is sufficient to give a clear title of sovereignty only when it is accompanied by actual possession. And this only applies of course to movables or to such immovables as are actually inclosed within fixed bounds and guarded. No such claim can be established in the present case, because the Portuguese maintain no garrisons in those regions. Neither can the Portuguese by any possible means claim to have discovered India, a country which was famous centuries and centuries ago! It was already known as early as the time of the emperor Augustus as the following quotation from Horace shows:

· "That worst of evils, poverty, to shun
· Dauntless through seas, and rocks, and fires you run
· To furthest Ind,"

And have not the Romans described for us in the most exact way the greater part of Ceylon? And as far as the other islands are concerned, not only the neighboring Persians and Arabs, but even Europeans, particularly the Venetians, knew them long before the Portuguese did.

But in addition to all this, discovery per se gives no legal rights over things unless before the alleged discovery they were res nullius. Now these Indians of the East, on the arrival of the Portuguese, although some of them were idolators, and some Mohammedans, and therefore sunk in grievous sin, had none the less perfect public and private ownership of their goods and possessions, from which they could not be dispossessed without just cause. The Spanish writer Victoria, following other writers of the highest

17

authority, has the most certain warrant for his conclusion that Christians, whether of the laity or of the clergy, cannot deprive infidels of their civil power and sovereignty merely on the ground that they are infidels, unless some other wrong has been done by them.

For religious belief, as Thomas Aquinas rightly observes, does not do away with either natural or human law from which sovereignty is derived. Surely it is a heresy to believe that infidels are not masters of their own property; consequently, to take from them their possessions on account of their religious belief is no less theft and robbery than it would be in the case of Christians.

Victoria then is right in saying that the Spaniards have no more legal right over the East Indians because of their religion, than the East Indians would have had over the Spaniards if they had happened to be the first foreigners to come to Spain. Nor are the East Indians stupid and unthinking; on the contrary they are intelligent and shrewd, so that a pretext for subduing them on the ground of their character could not be sustained. Such a pretext on its very face is an injustice. Plutarch said long ago that it was greed that furnished the pretext for conquering barbarous countries, and it is not unsuspected that greedy longing for the property of another often hid itself behind a pretext of civilizing barbarians. And now that well-known pretext of forcing nations into a higher state of civilization against their will, the pretext once monopolized by the Greeks and by Alexander the Great, is considered by all theologians, especially those of Spain, to be unjust and unholy.

CHAPTER III

The Portuguese have no right of sovereignty over the East Indies by virtue of title based on the Papal Donation

Next, if the partition made by the Pope Alexander VI is to be used by the Portuguese as authority for jurisdiction in the East Indies, then before all things else two points must be taken into consideration.

First, did the Pope merely desire to settle the disputes between the Portuguese and the Spaniards?

This was clearly within his power, inasmuch as he had been chosen to arbitrate between them, and in fact the kings of both countries had previously concluded certain treaties with each other on this very matter. Now if this be the case, seeing that the question concerns only the Portuguese and Spaniards, the decision of the Pope will of course not affect the other peoples of the world.

Second, did the Pope intend to give to two nations, each one third of the whole world?

But even if the Pope had intended and had had the power to make such a gift, still it would not have made the Portuguese sovereigns of those places. For it is not a donation that makes a sovereign, it is the consequent delivery of a thing and the subsequent possession thereof.

Now, if any one will scrutinize either divine or human law, not merely with a view to his own interests, he will easily apprehend that a donation of this kind, dealing with the property of others, is of no effect. I shall not enter here upon any discussion as to the power of the Pope, that is the

Bishop of the Roman Church, nor shall I advance anything but a hypothesis which is accepted by men of the greatest erudition, who lay the greatest stress on the power of the Pope, especially the Spaniards, who with their perspicacity easily see that our Lord Jesus Christ when he said "My kingdom is not of this world" thereby renounced all earthly power, and that while He was on earth as a man, He certainly did not have dominion over the whole world, and if He had had such dominion, still by no arguments could such a right be transferred to Peter, or be transmitted to the Roman Church by authority of the 'Vicar of Christ'; indeed, inasmuch as Christ had many things to which the Pope did not succeed, it has been boldly affirmed—and I shall use the very words of the writers—that the Pope is neither civil nor temporal Lord of the whole world. On the contrary, even if the Pope did have any such power on earth, still he would not be right in using it, because he ought to be satisfied with his own spiritual jurisdiction, and be utterly unable to grant that power to temporal princes. So then, if the Pope has any power at all, he has it, as they say, in the spiritual realm only. Therefore he has no authority over infidel nations, for they do not belong to the Church.

It follows therefore according to the opinions of Cajetan and Victoria and the more authoritative of the Theologians and writers on Canon Law, that there is no clear title against the East Indians, based either on the ground that the Pope made an absolute grant of those provinces as if he were their sovereign, or on the pretext that the East Indians do not recognize his sovereignty. Indeed, and in truth, it may be affirmed that no such pretext as that was ever invoked to despoil even the Saracens.

CHAPTER IV

The Portuguese have no right of sovereignty over the East Indies by title of war

Since it is clear, (as Victoria also says), from the refutation of any claim to title from the Pope's Donation, that the Spaniards when they sailed to those distant lands did not carry with them any right to occupy them as provinces, only one kind of title remains to be considered, namely, that based upon war. But even if this title could be justified, it would not serve to establish sovereignty, except by right of conquest, that is to say, occupation would be a prerequisite. But the Portuguese were as far as possible from occupation of those lands. They were not even at war with most of the peoples whom the Dutch visited. So therefore no legal claim could be established there by the Portuguese, because even if they had suffered wrongs from the East Indians, it might reasonably be considered by the long peace and friendly commercial relations that those injuries had been forgiven.

Indeed there was no pretext at all for going to war. For those who force war upon barbarous peoples, as the Spaniards did upon the aborigines of America, commonly allege one of two pretexts: either that they have been refused the right to trade, or that the barbarians are unwilling to acknowledge the doctrines of the True Faith. But as the Portuguese actually obtained from the East Indians the right to trade, they have, on that score at least, no grounds of complaint. Nor is there any better justification for the other pretext than the one alleged by the Greeks against the barbarians, to which Boëthius makes the following allusion:

· "Unjust and cruel wars they wage,
· And haste with flying darts the death to meet or deal.
· No right nor reason can they show;
· ' Tis but because their lands and laws are not the same."

Moreover the verdict of Thomas Aquinas, of the Council of Toledo, of Gregory, and of nearly all theologians, canonists, and jurists, is as follows: However persuasively and sufficiently the True Faith has been preached to the heathen—former subjects of Christian princes or apostates are quite another question—if they are unwilling to heed it, that is not sufficient cause to justify war upon them, or to despoil them of their goods.

It is worth while on this point to quote the actual words of Cajetan: 'There are some infidels who are neither in law nor in fact under the temporal jurisdiction of Christian princes; just as there were pagans who were never subjects of the Roman Empire, and yet who inhabit lands where the name of Christ was never heard. Now their rulers, though heathen, are legitimate rulers, whether the people live under a monarchical or a democratic régime. They are not to be deprived of sovereignty over their possessions because of their unbelief, since sovereignty is a matter of positive law, and unbelief is a matter of divine law, which cannot annual positive law, as has been argued above. In fact I know of no law against such unbelievers as regards their temporal possessions. Against them no King, no Emperor, not even the Roman Church, can declare war for the purpose of occupying their lands, or of subjecting them to temporal sway. For there is no just cause for war, since Jesus Christ the King of Kings, to whom all power was given in heaven and on earth, sent out for the conquest of the world not armed soldiers, but holy disciples, "as sheep in the midst of wolves." Nor do I read in the Old Testament, when possession had to be obtained by force of arms, that the Israelites waged war on any heathen land because of the unbelief of its inhabitants; but it was because the heathen refused them the right of innocent passage, or attacked them, as the Midianites did; or it was to recover the possessions which had been bestowed upon them by divine bounty. Wherefore we should be most miserable sinners if we should attempt to extend the religion of Jesus Christ by such means. Nor should we be their lawful rulers, but, on the contrary, we should be committing great robberies, and be compelled to make restitution as unjust conquerors and invaders. There must be sent to them as preachers, good men to convert them to God by their teaching and example; not men who will oppress them, despoil them, subdue and proselytize them, and "make them twofold more the children of hell than themselves," after the manner of the Pharisees'.

Indeed I have often heard that it has been decreed by the Council of Spain, and by the Churchmen, especially the Dominicans, that the Americans (Aztecs and Indians) should be converted to the Faith by the preaching of the Word alone, and not by war, and even that their liberty of which they had been robbed in the name of religion should be restored. This policy is said to have received the approval of Pope Paul III, and of Emperor Charles V, King of the Spains.

I pass over the fact that the Portuguese in most places do not further the extension of the faith, or indeed, pay any attention to it at all, since they are alive only to the acquisition of wealth. Nay, the very thing that is true of them, is the very thing which has been written of the Spaniards in America by a Spaniard, namely, that nothing is heard of miracles or wonders or examples of devout and religious life such as might convert others to the same faith, but on the other hand no end of scandals, of crimes, of impious deeds.

Wherefore, since both possession and a title of possession are lacking, and since the property and the sovereignty of the East Indies ought not to be considered as if they had previously been res nullius, and since, as they belong to the East Indians, they could not have been acquired legally by other persons, it follows that the East Indian nations in question are not the chattels of the Portuguese, but are free men and sui juris. This is not denied even by the Spanish jurists themselves.

CHAPTER V

Neither the Indian Ocean nor the right of navigation thereon belongs to the Portuguese by title of occupation

If therefore the Portuguese have acquired no legal right over the nations of the East Indies, and their territory and sovereignty, let us consider whether they have been able to obtain exclusive jurisdiction over the sea and its navigation or over trade. Let us first consider the case of the sea.

Now, in the legal phraseology of the Law of Nations, the sea is called indifferently the property of no one (res nullius), or a common possession (res communis), or public property (res publica). It will be most convenient to explain the signification of these terms if we follow the practice of all the poets since Hesiod, of the philosophers and jurists of the past, and distinguish certain epochs, the divisions of which are marked off perhaps not so much by intervals of time as by obvious logic and essential character. And we ought not to be criticised if in our explanation of a law deriving from nature, we use the authority and definition of those whose natural judgment admittedly is held in the highest esteem.

It is therefore necessary to explain that in the earliest stages of human existence both sovereignty and common possession had meanings other than those which they bear at the present time. For nowadays sovereignty means a particular kind of proprietorship, such in fact that it absolutely excludes like possession by any one else. On the other hand, we call a thing 'common' when its ownership or possession is held by several persons jointly according to a kind of partnership or mutual agreement from which all other persons are excluded. Poverty of language compels the use of the same words for things that are not the same. And so because of a certain similarity and likeness, our modern nomenclature is applied to that state of primitive law. Now, in ancient times, 'common' meant simply the opposite of 'particular'; and 'sovereignty' or 'ownership', meant the privilege of lawfully using common property. This seemed to the Scholastics to be a use in fact but not in law, because what now in law is called use, is a particular right, or if I may use their phraseology, is, in respect to other persons, a privative right.

In the primitive law of nations, which is sometimes called Natural Law, and which the poets sometimes portray as having existed in a Golden Age, and sometimes in the reign of Saturn or of Justice, there was no particular right. As Cicero says: 'But nothing is by nature private property'. And Horace: 'For nature has decreed to be the master of private soil neither him, nor me, nor anyone else'. For nature knows no sovereigns. Therefore in this sense we say that in those ancient times all things were held in common, meaning what the poets do when they say that primitive men acquired everything in common, and that Justice maintained a community of goods by means of an inviolable compact. And to make this clearer, they say that in those primitive times the fields were not delimited by boundary lines, and that there was no commercial intercourse. Avienus says: 'It seemed that all lands without distinction were common to all'.

The word 'seemed' is rightly added, owing to the changed meaning of the words, as we have noted above. But that kind of common possession relates to use, as is seen from a quotation from Seneca:

· "Every path was free,
· All things were used in common."

26

According to his reasoning there was a kind of sovereignty, but it was universal and unlimited. For God had not given all things to this individual or to that, but to the entire human race, and thus a number of persons, as it were en masse, were not debarred from being substantially sovereigns or owners of the same thing, which is quite contradictory to our modern meaning of sovereignty. For it now implies particular or private ownership, a thing which no one then had. Avienus has said very pertinently: 'All things belonged to him who had possession of them'.

It seems certain that the transition to the present distinction of ownerships did not come violently, but gradually, nature herself pointing out the way. For since there are some things, the use of which consists in their being used up, either because having become part of the very substance of the user they can never be used again, or because by use they become less fit for future use, it has become apparent, especially in dealing with the first category, such things as food and drink for example, that a certain kind of ownership is inseparable from use. For 'own' implies that a thing belongs to some one person, in such a way that it cannot belong to any other person. By the process of reasoning this was next extended to things of the second category, such as clothes and movables and some living things.

When that had come about, not even immovables, such, for instance, as fields, could remain unapportioned. For although their use does not consist merely in consumption, nevertheless it is bound up with subsequent consumption, as fields and plants are used to get food, and pastures to get clothing. There is, however, not enough fixed property to satisfy the use of everybody indiscriminately.

When property or ownership was invented, the law of property was established to imitate nature. For as that use began in connection with bodily needs, from which as we have said property first arose, so by a similar connection it was decided that things were the property of individuals. This is called 'occupation', a word most appropriate to those things which in former times had been held in common. It is this to which Seneca alludes in his tragedy Thyestes,

"Crime is between us to be seized by one."

And in one of his philosophical writings he also says: 'The equestrian rows of seats belong to all the equites; nevertheless, the seat of which I have taken possession is my own private place'. Further, Quintilian remarks that a thing which is created for all is the reward of industry, and Cicero says that things which have been occupied for a long time become the property of those who originally found them unoccupied.

This occupation or possession, however, in the case of things which resist seizure, like wild animals for example, must be uninterrupted or perpetually maintained, but in the case of other things it is sufficient if after physical possession is once taken the intention to possess is maintained. Possession of movables implies seizure, and possession of immovables either the erection of buildings or some determination of boundaries, such as fencing in. Hence Hermogenianus, in speaking of separate ownerships, adds the boundaries set to the fields and the buildings thereon constructed. This state of things is described thus by the poets Vergil and Ovid:

· "Then toils for beasts, and lime for birds, were found,"

· Then first men made homes.

· "Then landmarks limited to each his right,

· For all before was common as the light."

In still another place, as Hermogenianus points out, Ovid praises commerce, for the sake of which:

· 'Ships in triumph sail the unknown seas'.

At the same time, however, states began to be established, and so two categories were made of the things which had been wrested away from early ownership in common. For some things were public, that is, were the property of the people (which is the real meaning of that expression), while other things were private, that is, were the property of individuals. Ownership, however, both public and private, arises in the same way. On this point Seneca says: 'We speak in general of the land of the Athenians or the Campanians. It is the same land which again by means of private boundaries is divided among individual owners'. 'For each nation', Seneca says in another place, 'made its territories into separate kingdoms and built new cities'. Thus Cicero says: "On this principle the lands of Arpinum are said to belong to the Arpinates, the Tusculan lands to the Tusculans; and similar is the assignment of private property. Therefore, inasmuch as in each case some of those things which by nature had been common property became the property of individuals, each one should retain possession of that which has fallen to his lot." On the other hand Thucydides calls the land which in the division falls to no nation, ἀόριστος, that is, undefined, and undetermined by boundaries.

Two conclusions may be drawn from what has thus far been said. The first is, that that which cannot be occupied, or which never has been occupied, cannot be the property of any one, because all property has arisen from occupation. The second is, that all that which has been so constituted by nature that although serving some one person it still suffices for the common use of all other persons, is today and ought in perpetuity to remain in the same condition as when it was first created by nature. This is what Cicero meant when he wrote: "This then is the most comprehensive bond that unites together men as men and all to all; and under it the common right to all things that nature has produced for the common use of man is to be maintained." All things which can be used without loss to any one else come under this category. Hence, says Cicero, comes the well known prohibition: 'Deny no one the water that flows by'. For running water considered as such and not as a stream, is classed by the jurists among the things common to all mankind; as is done also by Ovid: 'Why do you deny me water? Its use is free to all. Nature has made neither sun nor air nor waves private property; they are public gifts'.

He says that these things are not by nature private possession, but that, as Ulpian claims, they are by nature things open to the use of all, both because in the first place they were produced by nature, and have never yet come under the sovereignty of any one, as Neratius says; and in the second place because, as Cicero says, they seem to have been created by nature for common use. But the poet uses 'public', in its usual meaning, not of those things which belong to any one people, but to human society as a whole; that is to say, things which are called 'public' are, according to the Laws of the law of nations, the common property of all, and the private property of none.

The air belongs to this class of things for two reasons. First, it is not susceptible of occupation; and second its common use is destined for all men. For the same reasons the sea is common to all, because it is so limitless that it cannot become a possession of any one, and because it is adapted for the use of all, whether we consider it from the point of view of navigation or of fisheries. Now, the same right which applies to the sea applies also to the things which the sea has carried away from other uses and made its own, such for example as the sands of the sea, of which the portion adjoining the land is called the coast or shore. Cicero therefore argues correctly: 'What is so common as the sea for those who are being tossed upon it, the shore for those who have been cast thereon'. Vergil also says that the air, the sea, and the shore are open to all men.

These things therefore are what the Romans call 'common' to all men by natural law, or as we have said, 'public' according to the law of nations; and indeed they call their use sometimes common, sometimes public. Nevertheless, although those things are with reason said to be res nullius, so far as private ownership is concerned, still they differ very much from those things which, though also res nullius, have not been marked out for common use, such for example as wild animals, fish, and birds. For if any one seizes those things and assumes possession of them, they can become objects of private ownership, but the things in the former category by the consensus of opinion of all mankind are forever exempt from such private ownership on account of their susceptibility to universal use; and as they belong to all they cannot be taken away from all by any one person any more than what is mine can be taken away from me by you. And Cicero says that one of the first gifts of Justice is the use of common property for common benefit. The Scholastics would define one of these categories as common in an affirmative, the other in a privative sense. This distinction is not only familiar to jurists, but it also expresses the popular belief. In

Athenaeus for instance the host is made to say that the sea is the common property of all, but that fish are the private property of him who catches them. And in Plautus' Rudens when the slave says: 'The sea is certainly common to all persons', the fisherman agrees; but when the slave adds: 'Then what is found in the common sea is common property', he rightly objects, saying: 'But what my net and hooks have taken, is absolutely my own'.

Therefore the sea can in no way become the private property of any one, because nature not only allows but enjoins its common use. Neither can the shore become the private property of any one. The following qualification, however, must be made. If any part of these things is by nature susceptible of occupation, it may become the property of the one who occupies it only so far as such occupation does not affect its common use. This qualification is deservedly recognized. For in such a case both conditions vanish through which it might eventuate, as we have said, that all of it would pass into private ownership.

Since therefore, to cite Pomponius, building is one kind of occupation, it is permissible to build upon the shore, if this can be done without inconvenience to other people; that is to say (I here follow Scaevola) if such building can be done without hindrance to public or common use of the shore. And whoever shall have constructed a building under the aforesaid circumstances will become the owner of the ground upon which said building is; because this ground is neither the property of any one else, nor is it necessary to common use. It becomes therefore the property of the occupier, but his ownership lasts no longer than his occupation lasts, inasmuch as the sea seems by nature to resist ownership. For just as a wild animal, if it shall have escaped and thus recovered its natural liberty, is no longer the property of its captor, so also the sea may recover its possession of the shore.

We have now shown that whatever by occupation can become private property can also become public property, that is, the private property of a whole nation. And so Celsus considered the shore included within the limits of the Roman Empire to be the property of the Roman people. There is not therefore the least reason for surprise that the Roman people through their emperors or praetors was able to grant to its subjects the right of occupying the shore. This public occupation, however, no less than private occupation, was subject to the restriction that it should not infringe on international rights. Therefore the Roman people could not forbid any one from having access to the seashore, and from spreading his fishing nets there to dry, and from doing other things which all men long ago decided were always permissible.

The nature of the sea, however, differs from that of the shore, because the sea, except for a very restricted space, can neither easily be built upon, nor inclosed; if the contrary were true yet this could hardly happen without hindrance to the general use. Nevertheless, if any small portion of the sea can be thus occupied, the occupation is recognized. The famous hyperbole of Horace must be quoted here: "The fishes note the narrowing of the waters by piers of rock laid in their depths."

Now Celsus holds that piles driven into the sea belong to the man who drove them. But such an act is not permissible if the use of the sea be thereby impaired. And Ulpian says that whoever builds a breakwater must see to it that it is not prejudicial to the interests of any one; for if this construction is likely to work an injury to any one, the injunction 'Nothing may be built on public property' would apply. Labeo, however, holds that in case any such construction should be made in the sea, the following injunction is to be enforced: 'Nothing may be built in the sea whereby the harbor, the roadstead, or the channel be rendered less safe for navigation'.

Now the same principle which applies to navigation applies also to fishing, namely, that it remains free and open to all. Nevertheless there shall be no prejudice if any one shall by fencing off with stakes an inlet of the sea make a fish pond for himself, and so establish a private preserve. Thus Lucullus once brought the water of the sea to his villa by cutting a tunnel through a mountain near Naples. I suspect too that the seawater reservoirs for fish mentioned by Varro and Columella were of this sort. And Martial had the same thing in mind when he says of the Formian villa of Apollinaris: 'Whenever Nereus feels the power of Aeolus, the table safe in its own resources laughs at the gale'. Ambrose also has something to say on the same subject: 'You bring the very sea into your estates that you may not lack for fish'. In the light of all this the meaning of Paulus is clear when he says that if any one has a private right over the sea, the rule uti possidetis applies. This rule however is applicable only to private suits, and not to public ones, among which are also to be included those suits which can be brought under the common law of nations. But here the question is one which concerns the right of use arising in a private suit, but not in a public or common one. For according to the authority of Marcianus whatever has been occupied and can be occupied is no longer subject to the law of nations as the sea is. Let us take an example. If any one had prevented Lucullus or Apollinaris from fishing in the private fish ponds which they had made by inclosing a small portion of the sea, according to the opinion of Paulus they would have the right of bringing an injunction, not merely an action for damages based on private ownership.

Indeed, if I shall have staked off such an inclosure in an inlet of the sea, just as in a branch of a river, and have fished there, especially if by doing so continuously for many years I shall have given proof of my intention to establish private ownership, I shall certainly prevent any one else from enjoying the same rights. I gather from Marcianus that this case is identical with that of the ownership of a lake, and it is true however long occupation lasts, as we have said above about the shore. But outside of an inlet this will not hold, for then the common use of the sea might be hindered.

Therefore if any one is prevented from fishing in front of my town house or country seat, it is a usurpation, but an illegal one, although Ulpian, who rather makes light of this usurpation, does say that if any one is so prevented he can bring an action for damages. The Emperor Leo, whose laws we do not use, contrary to the intent of the law, changed this, and declared that the entrances, or vestibules as it were, to the sea, were the private property of those who inhabited the shore, and that they had the right of fishing there. However he attached this condition, that the place should be occupied by certain jetty or pile constructions, such as the Greeks call ἐποχαί, thinking doubtless that no one who was himself allowed to fish anywhere in the sea would grudge any one else a small portion of it. To be sure it would be an intolerable outrage for any one to snatch away, even if he could do so, from public use a large area of the sea; an act which is justly reprehended by the Holy Man, who says: 'The lords of the earth claim for themselves a wide expanse of sea by jus mancipii, and they regard the right of fishing as a servitude over which their right is the same as that over their slaves. That gulf, says one, belongs to me, and that gulf to some one else. They divide the very elements among themselves, these great men'!

35

Therefore the sea is one of those things which is not an article of merchandise, and which cannot become private property. Hence it follows, to speak strictly, that no part of the sea can be considered as the territory of any people whatsoever. Placentinus seems to have recognized this when he said: 'The sea is a thing so clearly common to all, that it cannot be the property of any one save God alone'. Johannes Faber also asserts that the sea has been left sui juris, and remains in the primitive condition where all things were common. If it were otherwise there would be no difference between the things which are 'common to all', and those which are strictly termed 'public'; no difference, that is, between the sea and a river. A nation can take possession of a river, as it is inclosed within their boundaries, with the sea, they cannot do so.

Now, public territory arises out of the occupation of nations, just as private property arises out of the occupation of individuals. This is recognized by Celsus, who has drawn a sharp distinction between the shores of the sea, which the Roman people could occupy in such a way that its common use was not harmed, and the sea itself, which retained its primitive nature. In fact no law intimates a contrary view. Such laws as are cited by writers who are of the contrary opinion apply either to islands, which evidently could be occupied, or to harbors, which are not 'common', but 'public', that is, 'national'.

Now those who say that a certain sea belonged to the Roman people explain their statement to mean that the right of the Romans did not extend beyond protection and jurisdiction; this right they distinguish from ownership. Perchance they do not pay sufficient attention to the fact that although the Roman People were able to maintain fleets for the protection of navigation and to punish pirates captured on the sea, it was not done by private right, but by the common right which other free peoples also enjoy on the sea. We recognize, however, that certain peoples have agreed that pirates captured in this or in that part of the sea should come under the jurisdiction of this state or of that, and further that certain convenient limits of distinct jurisdiction have been apportioned on the sea. Now, this agreement does bind those who are parties to it, but it has no binding force on other nations, nor does it make the delimited area of the sea the private property of any one. It merely constitutes a personal right between contracting parties.

This distinction so conformable to natural reason is also confirmed by a reply once made by Ulpian. Upon being asked whether the owner of two maritime estates could on selling either of them impose on it such a servitude as the prohibition of fishing in a particular part of the sea, he replied that the thing in question, evidently the sea, could not be subjected to a servitude, because it was by nature open to all persons; but that since a contract made in good faith demands that the condition of a sale be respected, the present possessors and those who succeed to their rights were bound to observe that condition. It is true that the jurist is speaking of private estates and of private law, but in speaking here of the territory of peoples and of public law the same reasoning applies, because from the point of view of the whole human race peoples are treated as individuals.

Similarly, revenues levied on maritime fisheries are held to belong to the Crown, but they do not bind the sea itself or the fisheries, but only the persons engaged in fishing. Wherefore subjects, for whom a state or a ruler is by common consent competent to make laws, will perhaps be compelled to bear such charges, but so far as other persons are concerned the right of fishing ought everywhere to be exempt from tolls, lest a servitude be imposed upon the sea, which is not susceptible to a servitude.

The case of the sea is not the same as that of a river, for as a river is the property of a nation, the right to fish in it can be passed or leased by the nation or by the ruler, in such a way (and the like is true with the ancients) that the lessee enjoys the operation of the injunction de loco publico fruendo by virtue of the clause 'He who has the right to lease has leased the exclusive right of enjoyment'. Such a condition cannot arise in respect to the sea. Finally those who count fishing among the properties of the Crown have not examined carefully enough the very passage which they cite to prove their contention, as Isernia and Alvotus have noticed.

It has therefore been demonstrated that neither a nation nor an individual can establish any right of private ownership over the sea itself (I except inlets of the sea), inasmuch as its occupation is not permissible either by nature or on grounds of public utility. The discussion of this matter has been taken up for this reason, namely, that it may be seen that the Portuguese have not established private ownership over the sea by which people go to the East Indies. For the two reasons that stand in the way of ownership are in this case infinitely more powerful than in all others. That which in other cases seems difficult, is here absolutely impossible; and what in other cases we recognize as unjust is here most barbarous and inhuman.

The question at issue then is not one that concerns an INNER SEA, one which is surrounded on all sides by the land and at some places does not even exceed a river in breadth, although it is well known that the Roman jurists cited such an inner sea in their famous opinions condemning private avarice. No! the question at issue is the OUTER SEA, the OCEAN, that expanse of water which antiquity describes as the immense, the infinite, bounded only by the heavens, parent of all things; the ocean which the ancients believed was perpetually supplied with water not only by fountains, rivers, and seas, but by the clouds, and by the very stars of heaven themselves; the ocean which, although surrounding this earth, the home of the human race, with the ebb and flow of its tides, can be neither seized nor inclosed; nay, which rather possesses the earth than is by it possessed.

Further, the question at issue does not concern a gulf or a strait in this ocean, nor even all the expanse of sea which is visible from the shore. [But consider this!!] The Portuguese claim as their own the whole expanse of the sea which separates two parts of the world so far distant the one from the other, that in all the preceding centuries neither one has so much as heard of the other. Indeed, if we take into account the share of the Spaniards, whose claim is the same as that of the Portuguese, only a little less than the whole ocean is found to be subject to two nations, while all the rest of the peoples in the world are restricted to the narrow bounds of the northern seas. Nature was greatly deceived if when she spread the sea around all peoples she believed that it would also be adequate for the use of them all. If in a thing so vast as the sea a man were to reserve to himself from general use nothing more than mere sovereignty, still he would be considered a seeker after unreasonable power. If a man were to enjoin other people from fishing, he would not escape the reproach of monstrous greed. But the man who even prevents navigation, a thing which means no loss to himself, what are we to say of him?

If any person should prevent any other person from taking fire from his fire or a light from his torch, I should accuse him of violating the law of human society, because that is the essence of its very nature, as Ennius has said:

"No less shines his, when he his friend's hath lit."

Why then, when it can be done without any prejudice to his own interests, will not one person share with another things which are useful to the recipient, and no loss to the giver? These are services which the ancient philosophers thought ought to be rendered not only to foreigners but even rendered for nothing. But the same act which when private possessions are in question is jealousy can be nothing but cruelty when a common possession is in question. For it is most outrageous for you to appropriate a thing, which both by ordinance of nature and by common consent is as much mine as yours, so exclusively that you will not grant me a right of use in it which leaves it no less yours than it was before.

Nevertheless, even those who lay burdens upon foreigners, or appropriate things common to all, rely upon a possession which is to some extent real. For since original occupation created private property, therefore detention of a thing, though unjust, gives an appearance of ownership. But have the Portuguese completely covered the ocean, as we are wont to do on land, by laying out estates on it in such a way that they have the right to exclude from that ocean whom they will? Not at all! On the contrary, they are so far from having done so, that when they divide up the world to the disadvantage of other nations, they cannot even defend their action by showing any boundaries either natural or artificial, but are compelled to fall back upon some imaginary line. Indeed, if that were a recognized method, and such a delimitation of boundaries were sufficient to make possession valid, our geometers long since would have got possession of the face of the earth, our astronomers of the very skies.

But where in this case is that corporal possession or physical appropriation, without which no ownerships arise? There appears to be nothing truer than what our learned jurists have enunciated, namely, that since the sea is just as insusceptible of physical appropriation as the air, it cannot be attached to the possessions of any nation.

But if the Portuguese call occupying the sea merely to have sailed over it before other people, and to have, as it were, opened the way, could anything in the world be more ridiculous? For, as there is no part of the sea on which some person has not already sailed, it will necessarily follow that every route of navigation is occupied by some one. Therefore we peoples of today are all absolutely excluded. Why will not those men who have circumnavigated the globe be justified in saying that they have acquired for themselves the possession of the whole ocean! But there is not a single person in the world who does not know that a ship sailing through the sea leaves behind it no more legal right than it does a track. And as for the assumption of the Portuguese that no one has sailed that ocean before themselves, that is anything but true. For a great part of that sea near Morocco, which is in dispute, had already been navigated long before, and the sea as far east as the Arabian gulf has been made famous by the victories of Alexander the Great, as both Pliny and Mela tell us.

There is also much to substantiate the belief that the inhabitants of Cadiz were well acquainted long ago with this route, because when Gaius Caesar, the son of Augustus, held command in the Arabian gulf, pieces were found of shipwrecks recognized as Spanish. Caelius Antipater also has told us in his writings that he himself saw a Spaniard who had sailed from Spain to Ethiopia on a commercial voyage. Also the Arabians knew those seas, if the testimony of Cornelius Nepos is to be believed, because he says that in his own day a certain Eudoxus, fleeing from Lathyrus, king of Alexandria, sailed from the Arabian gulf and finally reached Cadiz. However, by far the most famous example is that of the Carthaginians. Those most famous mariners were well acquainted with that sea, because Hanno, when Carthage was at the height of her power, sailing from Cadiz to the farthest confines of Arabia, and doubling the promontory now known as the Cape of Good Hope (the ancient name seems to have been Hyperion Ceras), described in a book the entire route he had taken, the appearance of the coasts, and the location of the islands, declaring that at the farthest point he reached the sea had not yet given out but his provisions had.

Pliny's description of the route to the East, the embassies from the Indies to Augustus, and those from Ceylon to the emperor Claudius, and finally the accounts of the deeds of Trajan, and the writings of Ptolemaeus, all make it quite clear that in the days of Rome's greatest splendor voyages were made regularly from the Arabian gulf to India, to the islands of the Indian ocean, and even so far as to the golden Chersonesus, which many people think was Japan. Strabo says that in his own time a fleet of Alexandrian merchantmen set sail from the Arabian gulf for the distant lands of Ethiopia and India, although few ships had ever before attempted that voyage. The Roman people had a large revenue from the East. Pliny says that cohorts of archers were carried on the boats engaged in trade as protection against pirates; he states also that every year India alone paid into the Roman imperial treasury 500,000 sesterces, or 1,000,000 sesterces if the revenues from Arabia and China be added; further, that the merchandise brought from the East sold for one hundred times its original cost.

These examples cited from ancient times are sufficient proof that the Portuguese were not the first in that part of the world. Long before they ever came, every single part of that ocean had been long since explored. For how possibly could the Moors, the Ethiopians, the Arabians, the Persians, the peoples of India, have remained in ignorance of that part of the sea adjacent to their coasts!

Therefore they lie, who today boast that they discovered that sea.

Well then, some one will say, does it seem to be a matter of little moment that the Portuguese were the first to restore a navigation interrupted perhaps for many centuries, and unknown—as cannot be denied—at least to the nations of Europe, at great labor and cost and danger to themselves? On the contrary, if they had laid weight upon the fact that they were pointing out to all what they alone had rediscovered, there is no one so lacking in sense that he would not acknowledge the greatest obligation to them. For the Portuguese will have earned the same thanks, praise, and immortal glory with which all discoverers of great things have been content, whenever they have striven to benefit not themselves but the whole human race. But if the Portuguese had before their eyes only their own financial gain, surely their profit, which is always the largest for those first in a new field of enterprise, ought to have satisfied them. For we know that their first voyages returned a profit sometimes of forty times the original investment, and sometimes even more. And by this overseas trade it has come about that a people, previously for a long time poor, have leaped suddenly into the possession of great riches, and have surrounded themselves with such outward signs of luxurious magnificence as scarcely the most prosperous nations have been able to display at the height of their fortunes.

But if these Portuguese have led the way in this matter in order that no one may follow them, then they do not deserve any thanks, inasmuch as they have considered only their own profit. Nor can they call it their profit, because they are taking the profit of some one else. For it is not at all demonstrable that, if the Portuguese had not gone to the East Indies, no one else would have gone. For the times were coming on apace in which along with other sciences the geographical locations of seas and lands were being better known every day. The reports of the expeditions of the ancients mentioned above had aroused people, and even if all foreign shores had not been laid open at a single stroke as it were, yet they would have been brought to light gradually by sailing voyages, each new discovery pointing the way to the next. And so there would finally have been accomplished what the Portuguese showed could be done, because there were many nations with no less ardor than theirs to engage in commerce and to learn of foreign things. The Venetians, who already knew much about India, were ready to push their knowledge farther; the indefatigable zeal of the French of Brittany, and the boldness of the English would not have failed to make such an attempt; indeed the Dutch themselves have embarked upon much more desperate enterprises.

Therefore the Portuguese have neither just reason nor respectable authority to support their position, for all those persons who assume that the sea can be subjected to the sovereignty of any one assign it to him who holds in his power the nearest ports and the circumjacent shores. But in all that great extent of coast line reaching to the East Indies the Portuguese have nothing which they can call their own except a few fortified posts.

And then even if a man were to have dominion over the sea, still he could not take away anything from its common use, just as the Roman people could not prevent any one from doing on the shores of their dominions all those things which were permitted by the law of nations. And if it were possible to prohibit any of those things, say for example, fishing, for in a way it can be maintained that fish are exhaustible, still it would not be possible to prohibit navigation, for the sea is not exhausted by that use.

The most conclusive argument on this question by far however is the one that we have already brought forward based on the opinions of eminent jurists, namely, that even over land which had been converted into private property either by states or individuals, unarmed and innocent passage is not justly to be denied to persons of any country, exactly as the right to drink from a river is not to be denied. The reason is clear, because, inasmuch as one and the same thing is susceptible by nature to different uses, the nations seem on the one hand to have apportioned among themselves that use which cannot be maintained conveniently apart from private ownership; but on the other hand to have reserved that use through the exercise of which the condition of the owner would not be impaired.

It is clear therefore to every one that he who prevents another from navigating the sea has no support in law. Ulpian has said that he was even bound to pay damages, and other jurists have thought that the injunction utile prohibito could also be brought against him.

Finally, the relief prayed for by the Dutch rests upon a common right, since it is universally admitted that navigation on the sea is open to any one, even if permission is not obtained from any ruler. And this is specificially expressed in the Spanish laws.

CHAPTER VI

Neither the Sea nor the right of navigation thereon belongs to the Portuguese by virtue of title based on the Papal Donation

The Donation of Pope Alexander, inasmuch as the title based on discovery is seen to be deficient, may next be invoked by the Portuguese to justify their exclusive appropriation of the sea and the right of navigation thereon. But from what has been said above, that Donation is clearly convicted of being an act of empty ostentation. For a Donation has no effect on things outside the realm of trade. Wherefore since neither the sea nor the right of navigating it can become the private property of any man, it follows that it could not have been given by the Pope, nor accepted by the Portuguese. Besides, as has been mentioned above, following the opinion of all men of sound judgment, it is sufficiently well recognized that the Pope is not the temporal lord of the earth, and certainly not of the sea. Even if it be granted for the sake of argument that such were the case, still a right attaching to the Pontificate ought not to be transferred wholly or in part to any king or nation. Similarly no emperor could convert to his own uses or alienate at his own pleasure the provinces of his empire.

Now, inasmuch as no one concedes to the Pope in temporal matters a jus disponendi, except perhaps in so far as it is demanded by the necessity of spiritual matters, and inasmuch as the things now under discussion, namely, the sea and the right of navigating it, are concerned only with money and profits, not with piety, surely every one with any brains at all will agree that the Pope has no jurisdiction here. What of the fact that not even rulers, that is to say, temporal lords, can prohibit any one from navigation, since if they have any right at all upon the sea it is merely one of jurisdiction and protection! It is also a fact universally recognized that the Pope has no authority to commit acts repugnant to the law of nature. But it is repugnant to the law of nature, as we have already proved beyond a doubt, for any one to have as his own private property either the sea or its use. Finally, since the Pope is wholly unable to deprive any one of his own rights, what defense will there be for that Donation of his, if by a word he intended to exclude so many innocent, uncondemned, and guiltless nations from a right which belongs no less to them than to the Spaniards?

Therefore, either it must be affirmed that a pronunciamento of this sort has no force, or, as is no less credible, that it was the desire of the Pope to intercede in the quarrel between the Spaniards and the Portuguese, and that he had no concomitant intention of violating the rights of others.

CHAPTER VII

Neither the Sea nor the right of navigation thereon belongs to the Portuguese by title of prescription or custom

The last defense of injustice is usually a claim or plea based on prescription or on custom. To this defense therefore the Portuguese have resorted. But the best established reasoning of the law precludes them from enjoying the protection of either plea.

Prescription is a matter of municipal law; hence it cannot be applied as between kings, or as between free and independent nations. It has even less standing when it is in conflict with that which is always stronger than the municipal law, namely, the law of nature or nations. Nay, even municipal law itself prevents prescription in this case. For it is impossible to acquire by usucaption or prescription things which cannot become property, that is, which are not susceptible of possession or of quasi-possession, and which cannot be alienated. All of which is true with respect to the sea and its use.

And since public things, that is, things which are the property of a nation, cannot be acquired by mere efflux of time, either because of their nature, or because of the prerogatives of those against whom such prescription would act, is it not vastly more just that the benefits accruing from the enjoyment of common things should be given to the entire human race than to one nation alone? On this point Papinian has said: 'Prescription raised by long possession is not customarily recognized as valid in the acquisition of places known to international law as "public" '. As an example, to illustrate this point, he cites a shore some part of which had been occupied by means of a building constructed on it. But if this building should be destroyed, and some one else later should construct a building on the same spot, no exception could be taken to it. Then he illustrates the same point by the analogous case of a res publica. If, for example, any one has fished for many years in a branch of a river, and has then stopped fishing there, after that he cannot prevent any one else from enjoying the same right that he had.

Wherefore it appears that Angeli and his followers who have said that the Venetians and Genoese were able to acquire by prescription certain specific rights in the gulfs of the sea adjacent to their shores, either are mistaken, or are deceiving others; a thing which happens all too frequently with jurists when they exercise the authority of their sacred profession not for justice and law, but in order to gain the gratitude of the powerful. There is also an opinion of Marcianus, already cited above in another connection, which, when carefully compared with the words of Papinian, can have no other interpretation than the one formerly adopted by Johannes and Bartolus, and now accepted by all learned men, namely, that the jus prohibendi is in effect only while occupation lasts; it loses its force if occupation cease; and occupation once interrupted, even if it had been continuous for a thousand years, loses its rights, as Paul de Castro justly observes. And even if Marcianus had meant—which certainly was not in his mind at all—that acquisition by prescription is to be recognized wherever occupation is recognized, still it would have been absurd to apply what had been said about a public river to the common sea, or what had been said about an inlet or a river branch to a bay, since in the former case prescription would hinder the use of something common to all by the law of nations, and in the latter case would work no small injury to public use. Moreover, another argument brought forward by Angeli based on the use of aqueducts, has quite properly been rejected by every one, being, as de Castro pointed out, entirely aside from the point.

It is not true then that such prescription rises even at a time beyond the period of the memory of man. For since the law absolutely denies all prescription, not even immemorial time has any effect on the question; that is, as Felinus says, things imprescriptible by nature do not become prescriptible by the mere efflux of immemorial time. Balbus admits the truth of these arguments, but says that the opinion of Angeli is to be accepted on the ground that time immemorial is believed to have the same validity as prerogative for setting up a title, since a perfect title is presumed from such efflux of time. Hence it appears that the jurists thought if some part of a state, say of the Roman empire for example, at a period before the memory of man had exercised such a right, that a title by prescription would have to be admitted on that ground, exactly as if there had been a previous grant from a Prince. But inasmuch as there is no one who is sovereign of the whole human race with competence to grant to any man or to any nation such a right against all other men, with the annihilation of that pretext, title by prescription is also necessarily destroyed. Therefore the opinion of the jurists is that not even an infinite lapse of time is able to set up a right as between kings or independent nations.

Moreover Angeli brought forward a most foolish argument, affirming that even if prescription could not create ownership, still an exception ought to be made in favor of a possessor. Papinian however in unmistakable words says there is no exception, nor could he think otherwise, because in his day prescription was itself an exception. It is therefore true, as expressed also in the laws of Spain, that prescription based on no matter how immemorial a time, sets up no title to those things which are recognized as common to the use of mankind. One reason among others which can be given for this definition is that any one who uses a res communis does so evidently by virtue of common and not private right, and because of the imperfect character of possession he can therefore no more set up a legal title by prescription than can a usufructuary.

A second reason not to be overlooked is that although a title and good faith are presumed in a prescriptive right created by the efflux of immemorial time, nevertheless if it appears from the nature of the thing itself that no title at all can be established, and if thus there becomes evident bad faith—a thing held to be permanent in a nation as well as in an individual—then prescription fails because of a double defect. Also a third reason is that we have under consideration a merely facultative right which is not prescriptible, as we shall show below.

But there is no end to their subtilties. There are jurists who in this case would distinguish custom from prescription, so that if they are debarred from the one, they may fall back upon the other. But the distinction which they set up is most absurd. They say that the right of one person which is taken away from him is given to another by prescription; but that when any right is given to any one in such a way that it is not taken away from any one else, then it is called custom. As if indeed the right of navigation, which is common to all, upon being usurped by some one to the exclusion of all others, would not necessarily when it became the property of one be lost to all!

This error receives support from misinterpretation of what Paulus has to say about a private right of possession on the sea. Accursius said that such a right could be acquired by privilege or custom. But this addition which in no way agrees with the text of the jurist seems to be rather the interpretation of a mischievous guesser than of a faithful interpreter. The real meaning of the words of Paulus has been already explained. Besides, if more careful consideration had been given to the words of Ulpian which almost immediately precede those of Paulus, a very different assertion would have been made. For Ulpian acknowledges that if any one is prohibited from fishing in front of my house, such prohibition is a usurpation of right, allowed, it is true, by custom, but based on no law, and that an action for damages could not be denied the person thus prohibited from fishing.

He therefore condemns this practice, and calls it a usurpation; of the Christian jurists Ambrose does likewise, and both are right. For what is clearer than that custom is not valid when it is diametrically opposed to the law of nature or of nations? Indeed, custom is a sort of affirmative right, which cannot invalidate general or universal law. And it is a universal law that the sea and its use is common to all. Moreover what we have said about prescription applies with equal truth and force to custom; and if any one should investigate the opinions of those who have differed upon this matter, he would find no other opinion but that custom is established by privilege. No one has the power to confer a privilege which is prejudicial to the rights of the human race; wherefore such a custom has no force as between different states.

This entire question however has been most thoroughly treated by Vasquez, that glory of Spain, who leaves nothing ever to be desired when it comes to subtle examination of the law or to the exposition of the principles of liberty. He lays down this thesis: 'Places public and common to all by the law of nations cannot become objects of prescription'. This thesis he supports by many authorities, and then he subjoins the objections fabricated by Angeli and others, which we have enumerated above. But before examining these objections he makes the just and reasonable statement that the truth of all these matters depends upon a true conception both of the law of nature and the law of nations. For, since the law of nature arises out of Divine Providence, it is immutable; but a part of this natural law is the primary or primitive law of nations, differing from the secondary or positive law of nations, which is mutable. For if there are customs incompatible with the primary law of nations, then, according to the judgment of Vasquez, they are not customs belonging to men, but to wild beasts, customs which are corruptions and abuses, not laws and usages. Therefore those customs cannot become prescriptions by mere lapse of time, cannot be justified by the passage of any law, cannot be established by the consent, the protection, or the practice even of many nations. These statements he confirms by a number of examples, and particularly by the testimony of Alphonse de Castro the Spanish theologian.

'It is evident therefore', he says, 'how much to be suspected is the opinion of those persons mentioned above, who think that the Genoese or the Venetians can without injustice prohibit other nations from navigating the gulfs or bays of their respective seas, as if they had a prescriptive right to the very water itself. Such an act is not only contrary to the laws, but is contrary also to natural law or the primary law of nations, which we have said is immutable. And this is seen to be true because by that same law not only the seas or waters, but also all other immovables were res communes. And although in later times there was a partial abandonment of that law, in so far as concerns sovereignty and ownership of lands—which by natural law at first were held in common, then distinguished and divided, and thus finally separated from the primitive community of use;—nevertheless it was different as regards sovereignty over the sea, which from the beginning of the world down to this very day is and always has been a res communis, and which, as is well known, has in no wise changed from that status.

'And although', he continues, 'I have often heard that a great many Portuguese believe that their king has a prescriptive right over the navigation of the vast seas of the West Indies (probably the East Indies too) such that other nations are not allowed to traverse those waters; and although the common people among our own Spaniards seem to be of the same opinion, namely, that absolutely no one in the world except us Spaniards ourselves has the least right to navigate the great and immense sea which stretches to the regions of the Indies once subdued by our most powerful kings, as if that right has been ours alone by prescription; although, I repeat, I have heard both these things, nevertheless the belief of all those people is no less extravagantly foolish than that of those who are always cherishing the same delusions with respect to the Genoese and Venetians. Indeed the opinions of them all appear the more manifestly absurd, because no one of those nations can erect a prescription against itself; that is to say, not the Venetian republic, nor the Genoese republic, nor the kingdom of Spain nor of Portugal can raise prescriptions against rights they already possess by nature. For the one who claims a prescriptive right and the one who suffers by the establishment of such a claim must not be one and the same person.

'Against other nations they are even much less competent to raise a prescription, because the right of prescription is only a municipal right, as we have shown above at some length. Therefore such a right ceases to have any effect as between rulers or nations who do not recognize a superior in the temporal domain. For so far as the merely municipal laws of any place are concerned, they do not affect foreign peoples, nations, or even individuals, any more than if they did not exist or never had existed. Therefore it was necessary to have recourse to the common law of nations, primary as well as secondary, and to use a law which clearly had not admitted any such prescription and usurpation of the sea. For today the use of the waters is common, exactly as it has been since the creation of the world. Therefore no man has a right nor can acquire a right over the seas and waters which would be prejudicial to their common use. Besides, there is both in natural and divine law that famous rule: 'Whatsoever ye would that men should not do to you, do not ye even so to them'. Hence it follows, since navigation cannot harm any one except the navigator himself, it is only just that no one either can or ought to be interdicted therefrom, lest nature, free in her own realm, and least hurtful to herself, be found impeding the liberty of navigation, and thus offending against the accepted precept and rule that all things are supposed to be permitted which are not found expressly forbidden. Besides, not only would it be contrary to natural law to wish to prevent such free navigation, but we are even bound to do the opposite, that is, bound to assist such navigation in whatever way we can, when it can be done without any prejudice to ourselves'.

After Vasquez had established his point by the help of many authorities both human and divine, he added: 'It appears then, from what has gone before that the opinion held by Johannes Faber, Angeli, Baldus, and Franciscus Balbus, whom we have cited above, is not to be trusted, because they think that places common by the law of nations, even if not open to acquisition by prescription, can nevertheless be acquired by custom; but this is entirely false, and is a teaching which is both obscure and vague, which lacks the faintest glimmer of reasonableness, and which sets up a law in word but not in fact. For it is well established from the examples taken from the seas of the Spaniards, Portuguese, Venetians, Genoese, and others, that an exclusive right of navigation and a right of prohibiting others from navigation is no more to be acquired by custom than by prescription. And it is apparent that the reason is the same in both cases. And since according to the laws and reasons adduced above this would be contrary to natural equity and would not bring benefit but only injury, therefore as it could not be introduced by an express law, neither could it be introduced by a tacit or implied law, and that is what custom is. And far from justifying itself by any lapse of time, it rather becomes worse, and every day more injurious'.

Vasquez next shows that from the time of the earliest occupation of the earth every people possessed the right of hunting in its own territory, and of fishing in its own rivers. After those rights were once separated from the ancient community of rights in such a way that they admitted of particular attachments, they could be acquired by prescription based upon such an efflux of time that "the memory of its beginning does not exist," as if by the tacit permission of a nation. This comes about, however, by prescription and not by custom, because only the condition of him who acquires is bettered, while that of all other persons is made worse. Then after Vasquez had enumerated three conditions which are requisite in order that a private right of fishing in a river may become a right by prescription, he continues as follows:

'But what are we to say as regards the sea? There is more to say about it, because even the combination of the three conditions mentioned is not sufficient here for the acquisition of such a right. The reason for the difference between the sea on one hand and land and rivers on the other, is that in the case of the sea the same primitive right of nations regarding fishing and navigation which existed in the earliest times, still today exists undiminished and always will, and because that right was never separated from the community right of all mankind, and attached to any person or group of persons. But in the latter case, that of the land and rivers, it was different, as we have already set forth.

'But why, it is asked, does the secondary law of nations which brings about this separation when we consider lands and rivers cease to operate in the same way when we consider the sea? I reply, because in the former case it was expedient and necessary. For every one admits that if a great many persons hunt on the land or fish in a river, the forest is easily exhausted of wild animals and the river of fish, but such a contingency is impossible in the case of the sea. Again, the navigation of rivers is easily lessened and impeded by constructions placed therein, but this is not true of the sea. Again, a river is easily emptied by means of aqueducts but the sea cannot be emptied by any such means. Therefore there is not equal reason on both sides.

'Neither does what we have said above about the common use of waters, springs, and rivers, apply in this case, for common use is recognized in them all for purposes of drinking and the like, such usages namely as do not injure at all or in the slightest degree him who owns a river or has some other right in one. These are trifles for which we have no time. What makes for our contention is the fact that no lapse of time will give a prescriptive right to anything unjust. Therefore an unjust law is not capable of erecting a prescriptive right or of being justified by efflux of time'. A little farther on Vasquez says: 'Things which are imprescriptible by the disposition of the law, may not become objects of prescription even after the lapse of a thousand years'. This statement he supports by countless citations from the jurists.

Every one perceives that no usurpation no matter how long continued is competent to intercept the use of a res communis. And it must also be added, that the authority of those who hold dissenting opinions cannot possibly be applied to the question here at issue. For they are talking about the Mediterranean, we are talking about the Ocean; they speak of a gulf, we of the boundless sea; and from the point of view of occupation these are wholly different things. And too, those peoples, to whom the authorities just mentioned concede prescription, the Venetians and Genoese for example, possess a continuous shore line on the sea, but it is clear that not even that kind of possession can be claimed for the Portuguese.

Further, even if mere lapse of time, as some think, could establish a right by prescription over public property, still the conditions absolutely indispensable for the creation of such a right are in this case absent. The conditions demanded are these: first, all jurists teach that he who sets up a prescriptive right of this sort shall have been in actual possession not only for a considerable period, but from time immemorial; next, that during all that time no one else shall have exercised the same right of possession unless by permission of that possessor or clandestinely; besides that, it is necessary that he shall have prevented other persons wishing to use his possession from so doing, and that such measures be a matter of common knowledge and done by the suffrance of those concerned in the matter. For even if he had continuously exercised his right of possession, and had always prevented from using his possession some of those who wished to do so, but not all; then, because some had been prevented from exercising and others freely allowed to exercise that use, that kind of possession according to the opinion of the jurists, is not sufficient to establish a right by prescription.

It is clear therefore that all these conditions should be present, both because law is opposed to the prescription of public things, and in order that he who sets up such a prescription may seem to have used his own private right, not a public right, and that too by continuous possession.

Now, inasmuch as time beyond the period of the memory of man is demanded for the creation of a prescriptive right, it is not always sufficient, as the best commentators point out, to prove the lapse of a hundred years, but as no one would be alive who had seen or heard the contrary, the tradition handed down to us by our ancestors ought to be undisputed. It was during the reign of King John, in the year of our Lord 1477, at the time of the wars in Africa, that the Portuguese began to push their discoveries first into the more distant parts of the Ocean. Twenty years later, during the reign of King Emmanuel, they rounded the Cape of Good Hope, and somewhat later yet, reached Malacca, and the islands beyond, the very islands, indeed, to which the Dutch began to sail in the year 1595, that is, well within a hundred years of the time that the Portuguese first arrived. And in truth even in that interval, the usurpation of rights there by other parties had interrupted the competence of everybody else to create a prescriptive right. For example, from the year 1519, the Spaniards rendered the possession by the Portuguese of the sea around the Malaccas a very uncertain one. Even the French and English made their way to those newly discovered places not secretly, but by force of arms. And besides these, the inhabitants of the entire coast of Africa and Asia constantly used for fishing and navigation that part of the sea nearest their own several coasts, and were never interdicted from such use by the Portuguese.

The conclusion of the whole matter therefore is that the Portuguese are in possession of no right whereby they may interdict to any nation whatsoever the navigation of the Ocean to the East Indies.

CHAPTER VIII

By the Law of Nations trade is free to all persons whatsoever

If however the Portuguese claim that they have an exclusive right to trade with the East Indies, their claim will be refuted by practically all the same arguments which already have been brought forward. Nevertheless I shall repeat them briefly, and apply them to this particular claim.

By the law of nations the principle was introduced that the opportunity to engage in trade, of which no one can be deprived, should be free to all men. This principle, inasmuch as its application was continually necessary after the distinctions of private ownerships were made, can therefore be seen to have had a very remote origin. Aristotle, in a very clever phrase, in his work entitled the Politics, has said that the art of exchange is a completion of the independence which Nature requires. Therefore trade ought to be common to all according to the law of nations, not only in a negative but also in a positive, or as the jurists say, affirmative sense. The things that come under the former category are subject to change, those of the latter category are not. This statement is to be explained in the following way.

Nature had given all things to all men. But since men were prevented from using many things which were desirable in every day life because they lived so far apart, and because, as we have said above, everything was not found everywhere, it was necessary to transport things from one place to another; not that there was yet an interchange of commodities, but that people were accustomed to make reciprocal use of things found in one another's territory according to their own judgment. They say that trade arose among the Chinese in about this way. Things were deposited at places out in the desert and left to the good faith and conscience of those who exchanged things of their own for what they took.

But when movables passed into private ownership (a change brought about by necessity, as has been explained above), straightway there arose a method of exchange by which the lack of one person was supplemented by that of which another person had an over supply. Hence commerce was born out of necessity for the commodities of life, as Pliny shows by a citation from Homer. But after immovables also began to be recognized as private property, the consequent annihilation of universal community of use made commerce a necessity not only between men whose habitations were far apart but even between men who were neighbors; and in order that trade might be carried on more easily, somewhat later they invented money, which, as the derivation of the word shows, is a civic institution.

Therefore the universal basis of all contracts, namely exchange, is derived from nature; but some particular kinds of exchange, and the money payment itself, are derived from law; although the older commentators on the law have not made this distinction sufficiently clear. Nevertheless all authorities agree that the ownership of things, particularly of movables, arises out of the primary law of nations, and that all contracts in which a price is not mentioned, are derived from the same source. The philosophers distinguish two kinds of exchange using Greek words which we shall take the liberty to translate as 'wholesale' and 'retail' trade. The former, as the Greek word shows, signifies trade or exchange between widely separated nations, and it ranks first in the order of Nature, as is shown in Plato's Republic.

The latter seems to be the same kind of exchange that Aristotle calls by another Greek word which means retail or shop trade between citizens. Aristotle makes a further division of wholesale trade into overland and overseas trade. But of the two, retail trade is the more petty and sordid, and wholesale the more honorable; but most honorable of all is the wholesale overseas trade, because it makes so many people sharers in so many things.

Hence Ulpian says that the maintenance of ships is the highest duty of a state, because it is an absolutely natural necessity, but that the maintenance of hucksters has not the same value. In another place Aristotle says: "For the art of exchange extends to all possessions, and it arises at first in a natural manner from the circumstance that some have too little, others too much." And Seneca is also to be cited in this connection for he has said that buying and selling is the law of nations.

Therefore freedom of trade is based on a primitive right of nations which has a natural and permanent cause; and so that right cannot be destroyed, or at all events it may not be destroyed except by the consent of all nations. So far is that from being the case, that any one nation may justly oppose in any way, any other two nations that desire to enter into a mutual and exclusive contractual relation.

CHAPTER IX

Trade with the East Indies does not belong to the Portuguese by title of occupation

Neither discovery nor occupation [which have been fully treated in Chapters II and V], is to be invoked on the point here under consideration, because the right of carrying on trade is not something corporal, which can be physically seized; nor would discovery or occupation help the case of the Portuguese even if they had been the very first persons to trade with the East Indies, although such a claim would be entirely untenable and false. For since in the beginning peoples set out along different paths, it was necessary that some become the first traders, nevertheless it is absolutely certain that those traders did not on that account acquire any rights. Wherefore if the Portuguese have any right by virtue of which they alone may trade with the East Indies, that right like other servitudes ought to arise from concession, either express or tacit, that is to say, from prescription. Otherwise no such right can exist.

CHAPTER X

Trade with the East Indies does not belong to the Portuguese by virtue of title based on the Papal Donation

No one has granted it except perhaps the Pope, and he did not have the power. For no one can give away what he does not himself possess. But the Pope, unless he were the temporal master of the whole world, which sensible men deny, cannot say that the universal right in respect of trade belongs to him. Especially is this true since trade has to do only with material gains, and has no concern at all with spiritual matters, outside of which, as all admit, Papal power ceases. Besides, if the Pope wished to give that right to the Portuguese alone, and to deprive all other men of the same right, he would be doing a double injustice. In the first place, he would do an injustice to the people of the East Indies who, placed as we have said outside the Church, are in no way subjects of the Pope. Therefore, since the Pope cannot take away from them anything that is theirs, he could not take away their right of trading with whomsoever they please. In the second place, he would do an injustice to all other men both Christian and non-Christian, from whom he could not take that same right without a hearing. Besides, what are we to say of the fact that not even temporal lords in their own dominions are competent to prohibit the freedom of trade, as has been demonstrated above by reasonable and authoritative statements?

Therefore it must be acknowledged, that the authority of the Pope has absolutely no force against the eternal law of nature and of nations, from whence came that liberty which is destined to endure for ever and ever.

CHAPTER XI

Trade with the East Indies does not belong to the Portuguese by title of prescription or custom

Last of all, prescription, or if you prefer the term, custom. We have shown that according to Vasquez, neither prescription nor custom had any force as between free nations or the rulers of different peoples, or any force against those principles which were introduced by primitive law. And here as before, mere efflux of time does not bring it to pass that the right of trade, which does not partake of the nature of ownership, becomes a private possession. Now in this case neither title nor good faith can be shown, and inasmuch as good faith is clearly absent, according to legal rules prescription will not be called a right, but an injury.

Nay, the very possession involved in trading seems not to have arisen out of a private right, but out of a public right which belongs equally to all; so on the other hand, because nations perhaps neglected to trade with the East Indies, it must not be presumed that they did so as a favor to the Portuguese, but because they believed it to be to their own best interests. But nothing stands in their way, when once expediency shall have persuaded them, to prevent them from doing what they had not previously done. For the jurists have handed down as incontestable the principle that where things arbitrable or facultative are such that they produce nothing more than the facultative act per se, but do not create a new right, that in all such cases not even a thousand years will create a title by prescription or custom. This, as Vasquez points out, acts both affirmatively and negatively. For I am not compelled to do what I have hitherto done of my own free will, nor am I compelled to stop doing what I have never done.

What moreover could be more absurd then to deduce from the fact that we as individuals are not able always to conclude a bargain with other individuals, that there is not preserved to us for the future the right of bargaining with them if opportunity shall have offered? The same Vasquez has also most justly said that not even the lapse of infinite time establishes a right which seems to have arisen from necessity rather than choice.

Therefore in order to establish a prescriptive right to the trade with the East Indies the Portuguese would be compelled to prove coercion. But since in such a case as this coercion is contrary to the law of nature and obnoxious to all mankind, it cannot establish a right. Next, that coercion must needs have been in existence for so long a time that "the memory of its beginning does not exist"; that, however, is so far from being the case that not even a hundred years had elapsed since the Venetians controlled nearly the entire trade with the East Indies, carrying it via Alexandria. Again, the coercion ought to have been such that it was not resisted; but the English and the French and other nations besides, did resist it. Finally, it is not sufficient that some be coerced, but it is indispensable that all be coerced, because the possession of freedom of trade is preserved to all by a failure to use coercion upon even one person. Moreover, the Arabians and the Chinese are at the present day still carrying on with the people of the East Indies a trade which has been uninterrupted for several centuries.

Portuguese usurpation is worthless.

CHAPTER XII

The Portuguese prohibition of trade has no foundation in equity

From what has been said thus far it is easy to see the blind cupidity of those who in order not to admit any one else to a share in their gains, strive to still their consciences by the very arguments which the Spanish jurists, interested too in the same case, show to be absolutely empty. For they intimate as clearly as they can that as regards India all the pretexts employed, are far fetched and unjust. They add that this right was never seriously approved by the swarm of theologians. Indeed, what is more unjust than the complaint made by the Portuguese that their profits are drained off by a freedom which is incompatible with their license? An incontrovertible rule of law lays down that a man who uses his own right is justly presumed to be contriving neither a deceit nor a fraud, in fact not even to be doing any one an injury. This is particularly true, if he has no intention to harm any one, but only to increase his own property. For what ought to be considered is the chief and ultimate intent not the irrelevant consequence. Indeed, if we may with propriety agree with Ulpian, he is not doing an injury, but he is preventing some one from getting a profit which another was previously enjoying.

Moreover it is natural and conformable to the highest law as well as equity, that when a gain open to all is concerned every person prefers it for himself rather than for another, even if that other had already discovered it. Who would countenance an artisan who complained that another artisan was taking away his profits by the exercise of the same craft? But the cause of the Dutch is the more reasonable, because their advantage in this matter is bound up with the advantage of the whole human race, an advantage which the Portuguese are trying to destroy. Nor will it be correct to say, that this is done in rivalry, as Vasquez shows in a similar case. For clearly we must either deny or affirm that this is done not only in honorable but in most honorable rivalry, and, according to Hesiod, 'This rivalry is honorable for mortal men'. For, says Vasquez, if any one should be so moved by love for his fellow men that he sells grain in hard times for a lower price than usual, he would diminish the wicked oppression of those men who in the same season of cruel financial stringency would have sold their grain at a higher price than usual. But, some one will object, by such methods the profits of others will be made less. 'We do not deny it', says Vasquez, 'but they are made less to the corresponding advantage of all other men. And would that the profits of all Rulers and Tyrants of this world could be thus lessened'!

Indeed can anything more unjust be conceived than for the Spaniards to hold the entire world tributary, so that it is not permissible either to buy or to sell except at their good pleasure? In all states we heap odium upon grain speculators and even bring them to punishment; and in very truth there seems to be no other sort of business so disgraceful as that of forcing up prices in the grain market. That is not to be wondered at, for such speculators are doing an injury to nature, who, as Aristotle says, is fertile for all alike. Accordingly it ought not to be supposed that trade was invented for the benefit of a few, but in order that the lack of one would be counterbalanced by the oversupply of another, a fair return also being guaranteed to all who take upon themselves the work and the danger of transport.

Is the same thing then which is considered grievous and pernicious in the smaller community of a state to be put up with at all in that great community of the human race? Shall the people of Spain, forsooth, assume a monopoly of all the world? Ambrose inveighs against those who interfere with the freedom of the sea; Augustine against those who obstruct the overland routes; and Gregory of Nazianzus against those who buy goods and hold them, and thus (as he eloquently says) make profits for themselves alone out of the helplessness and need of others. Indeed in the opinion of this wise and holy man any person who holds back grain and thus forces up the market price ought to be given over to public punishment and be adjudged worthy of death.

Therefore the Portuguese may cry as loud and as long as they shall please: 'You are cutting down our profits'! The Dutch will answer: 'Nay! we are but looking out for our own interests! Are you angry because we share with you in the winds and the sea? Pray, who had promised that you would always have those advantages? You are secure in the possession of that with which we are quite content'.

CHAPTER XIII

The Dutch must maintain their right of trade with the East Indies by peace, by treaty, or by war

Wherefore since both law and equity demand that trade with the East Indies be as free to us as to any one else, it follows that we are to maintain at all hazards that freedom which is ours by nature, either by coming to a peace agreement with the Spaniards, or by concluding a treaty, or by continuing the war. So far as peace is concerned, it is well known that there are two kinds of peace, one made on terms of equality, the other on unequal terms. The Greeks call the former kind a compact between equals, the latter an enjoined truce; the former is meant for high souled men, the latter for servile spirits. Demosthenes in his speech on the liberty of the Rhodians says that it was necessary for those who wished to be free to keep away from treaties which were imposed upon them, because such treaties were almost the same as slavery. Such conditions are all those by which one party is lessened in its own right, according to the definition of Isocrates. For if, as Cicero says, wars must be undertaken in order that people may live in peace unharmed, it follows that peace must be called not a pact which entails slavery but which brings undisturbed liberty, especially as peace and justice according to the opinion of many philosophers and theologians differ more in name than in fact, and as peace is a harmonious agreement based not on individual whim, but on well ordered regulations.

If however a truce is arranged for, it is quite clear from the very nature of a truce, that during its continuance no one's condition ought to change for the worse, inasmuch as both parties stand on the equivalent of a uti possidetis.

But if we are driven into war by the injustice of our enemies, the justice of our cause ought to bring hope and confidence in a happy outcome. "For," as Demosthenes has said, "every one fights his hardest to recover what he has lost; but when men endeavor to gain at the expense of others it is not so." The Emperor Alexander has expressed his idea in this way: 'Those who begin unjust deeds, must bear the greatest blame; but those who repel aggressors are twice armed, both with courage because of their just cause, and with the highest hope because they are not doing a wrong, but are warding off a wrong'.

Therefore, if it be necessary, arise, O nation unconquered on the sea, and fight boldly, not only for your own liberty, but for that of the human race. "Nor let it fright thee that their fleet is winged, each ship, with an hundred oars. The sea whereon it sails will have none of it. And though the prows bear figures threatening to cast rocks such as Centaurs throw, thou shalt find them but hollow planks and painted terrors. 'Tis his cause that makes or mars a soldier's strength. If the cause be not just, shame strikes the weapon from his hands."

If many writers, Augustine himself among them, believed it was right to take up arms because innocent passage was refused across foreign territory, how much more justly will arms be taken up against those from whom the demand is made of the common and innocent use of the sea, which by the law of nature is common to all? If those nations which interdicted others from trade on their own soil are justly attacked, what of those nations which separate by force and interrupt the mutual intercourse of peoples over whom they have no rights at all? If this case should be taken into court, there can be no doubt what opinion ought to be anticipated from a just judge. The praetor's law says: 'I forbid force to be used in preventing any one from sailing a ship or a boat on a public river, or from unloading his cargo on the bank'. The commentators say that the injunction must be applied in the same manner to the sea and to the seashore. Labeo, for example, in commenting on the praetor's edict, 'Let nothing be done in a public river or on its bank, by which a landing or a channel for shipping be obstructed', said there was a similar interdict which applied to the sea, namely, 'Let nothing be done on the sea or on the seashore by which a harbor, a landing, or a channel for shipping be obstructed'.

Now after this explicit prohibition, if any one be prevented from navigating the sea, or not allowed to sell or to make use of his own wares and products, Ulpian says that he can bring an action for damages on that ground. Also the theologians and the casuists agree that he who prevents another from buying or selling, or who puts his private interests before the public and common interests, or who in any way hinders another in the use of something which is his by common right, is held in damages to complete restitution in an amount fixed by an honorable arbitrator.

Following these principles a good judge would award to the Dutch the freedom of trade, and would forbid the Portuguese and others from using force to hinder that freedom, and would order the payment of just damages. But when a judgment which would be rendered in a court cannot be obtained, it should with justice be demanded in a war. Augustine acknowledges this when he says: 'The injustice of an adversary brings a just war'. Cicero also says: "There are two ways of settling a dispute; first, by discussion; second, by physical force; we must resort to force only in case we may not avail ourselves of discussion." And King Theodoric says: 'Recourse must then be had to arms when justice can find no lodgment in an adversary's heart'. Pomponius, however, has handed down a decision which has more bearing on our argument than any of the citations already made. He declared that the man who seized a thing common to all to the prejudice of every one else must be forcibly prevented from so doing. The theologians also say that just as war is righteously undertaken in defense of individual property, so no less righteously is it undertaken in behalf of the use of those things which by natural law ought to be common property. Therefore he who closes up roads and hinders the export of merchandise ought to be prevented from so doing via facti, even without waiting for any public authority.

Since these things are so, there need not be the slightest fear that God will prosper the efforts of those who violate that most stable law of nature which He himself has instituted, or that even men will allow those to go unpunished who for the sake alone of private gain oppose a common benefit of the human race.

APPENDIX

Two letters of Philip III, King of Spain

As several letters of the King of Spain have come of late into our hands, in which his design and that of the Portuguese is clearly disclosed, it seemed worth while to translate into Latin two of them which had particular bearing upon the controversy at issue, and to append them here.

LETTER I

To Don Martin Alphonse de Castro, our beloved viceroy, I, the King, send many greetings:

Together with this letter will come to you a copy printed in type of an edict which I have taken much pains to draw up, by which, for reasons which you will see expressed, and for other reasons which are consonant with my interests, I prohibit all commerce of foreigners in India itself, and in all other regions across the seas. As this matter is of the greatest importance and serviceableness, and ought to be carried out with the highest zeal, I command you, as soon as you shall have received this letter and edict, to further with all diligence its publication in all places and districts under your jurisdiction, and to carry out the provisions of the edict without exception of any person whatsoever, no matter what his quality, age, or condition, and without delay and excuse, and to proceed to the fulfilment of this command with the full power of your authority, no delay, appeal, or obstacle to the contrary, being admitted, of any kind, sort, or quality.

Therefore I order that this duty be discharged by those officers to whom its execution belongs, and that they be informed that not only will those who disobey serve me ill, but that I will punish them by depriving them of the offices in which they now serve me.

Further, inasmuch as it has been reported to me that within your jurisdiction there are sojourning many foreigners of different nations, Italians, French, Germans, and men of the Low Countries, the larger part of whom as we know came there by way of Persia and Turkey, and not through our realm; and inasmuch as, if this edict be rigidly enforced against those persons to the letter, some inconveniences might follow, if they should escape to the Moors, our enemies, and make known to our neighbors the disposition of my forces, and thus show ways that they might be able to harm my dominion: Therefore, I wish you to carry out the provisions of this edict as the exigencies of circumstances and occasion demand, and to use all prudence necessary in order to avoid those difficulties, taking especial pains to keep all foreigners in your power, and to guard them in accordance with their individual rank, so that they may have no opportunity to attempt anything prejudicial to our power, that thus I may attain fully that end which I have set forth in this edict.

Given at Lisbon, on the 28th of November in the year of our Lord, 1606. Signed by the king, and addressed: For the king, to Don Martin Alphonso de Castro, his Councillor, and Viceroy for the East Indies.

Since the month of August, 1914, the expression "Freedom of the Seas" has been on the lips alike of belligerent and neutral, and it seems as advisable as it is timely to issue— for the first time in English—the famous Latin tractate of Grotius proclaiming, explaining, and in no small measure making the "freedom of the seas."

The title of the little book, first published, anonymously, in November, 1608, explains the reason for its composition: "The Freedom of the Seas, or the Right which belongs to the Dutch to take part in the East Indian trade." It was an open secret that it was written by the young Dutch scholar and lawyer, Hugo Grotius. It was a secret and remained a secret until 1868 that the Mare Liberum was none other than Chapter XII of the treatise De Jure Praedae, written by Grotius in the winter of 1604–5, which first came to light in 1864 and was given to the world four years later.

The publication of the treatise on the law of prize is important as showing that the author of the Mare Liberum was already an accomplished international lawyer, and it proves beyond peradventure that the masterpiece of 1625 on the "Law of War and Peace" was not a hurried production, but the culmination of study and reflection extending over twenty years and more. More important still is the fact that neither the law of prize nor the Mare Liberum was a philosophic exercise, for it appears that Grotius had been retained by the Dutch East India Company to justify the capture by one of its ships of a Portuguese galleon in the straits of Malacca in the year 1602; that the treatise on the law of prize, of which the Mare Liberum is a chapter, was in the nature of a brief; and that the first systematic treatise on the law of nations—The Law of War and Peace—was not merely a philosophical disquisition, but that it was the direct outgrowth of an actual case and of professional employment.

The Spaniards, as is well known, then claimed the Pacific Ocean and the Gulf of Mexico, and Portugal claimed, in like manner, the Atlantic south of Morocco and the Indian Ocean, and both nations, at this time under a common sovereign, claimed and sought to exercise the right of excluding all foreigners from navigating or entering these waters. The Dutch, then at war with Spain, although not technically at war with Portugal, established themselves in 1598 in the island of Mauritius. Shortly thereafter they made settlements in Java and in the Moluccas. In 1602 the Dutch East India Company was formed, and, as it attempted to trade with the East Indies, its vessels came into competition with those of the Portuguese engaged in the Eastern trade, which sought to exclude them from the Indian waters. One Heemskerck, a captain in the employ of the Company, took a large Portuguese galleon in the Straits of Malacca. To trade with the East Indies was one thing, to capture Portuguese vessels was quite another thing. Therefore, some members of the Company refused their parts of the prize; others sold their shares in the company, and still others thought of establishing a new company in France, under the protection of King Henry IV, which should trade in peace and abstain from all warlike action. The matter was therefore one of no little importance, and it appears that Grotius was consulted and wrote his treatise on the law of prize, which is in the nature of a brief and is, at any rate, a lawyer's argument.

It will be observed that the Mare Liberum was written to refute the unjustified claims of Spain and Portugal to the high seas and to exclude foreigners therefrom. The claims of England, less extensive but not less unjustifiable, were not mentioned, and yet, if the arguments of Grotius were sound, the English claims to the high seas to the south and east of England, as well as to undefined regions to the north and west, would likewise fall to the ground. Therefore the distinguished English lawyer, scholar, and publicist, John Selden by name, bestirred himself in behalf of his country and wrote his Mare Clausum in 1617 or 1618, although it was not published until 1635, to refute the little tractate, Mare Liberum. In the dedication to King Charles I, Selden said: "There are among foreign writers, who rashly attribute your Majesty's more southern and eastern sea to their princes. Nor are there a few, who following chiefly some of the ancient Caesarian lawyers, endeavor to affirm, or beyond reason too easily admit, that all seas are common to the universality of mankind." The thesis of Selden was twofold: first, "that the sea, by the law of nature or nations, is not common to all men, but capable of private dominion or property as well as the land"; second, "that the King of Great Britain is lord of the sea flowing about, as an inseparable and perpetual appendant of the British Empire."

LETTER II

To our beloved viceroy, I, the King send many greetings:

Although I consider it absolutely certain that your presence and the forces which you took with you into those Eastern regions, guarantee that our enemies, the Dutch, who infest those quarters as well as the natives who give them a welcome reception, will be so thoroughly punished that neither the one nor the other will ever dare such practices in the future: still it will be expedient for the protection of our interests, that, when you shall return to Goa, you leave in those parts of the sea a fleet large and capable enough to do the business, and also that you delegate the supreme command of that fleet to Andrea Hurtado de Mendoza, or to any one else whom you shall consider better fitted for this post. I rely upon your affection for me, knowing that in this matter you will do nothing but what will be most useful to my interests.

Given at Madrid the 27th day of January in the year of our Lord 1607. Signed by the king, and addressed: For the king, to Don Martin Alfonso de Castro, his Councillor, and Viceroy for the East Indies.

Made in the USA
Middletown, DE
17 September 2020